A C

Because you are but a young man, beware of temptations and snares; and above all, be careful to keep yourself in the use of means; resort to good company; and howbeit you be nicknamed a Puritan, and mocked, yet care not for that, but rejoice and be glad, that they who are scorned and scoffed by this godless and vain world, and nicknamed Puritans, would admit you to their society; for I must tell you, when I am at this point as you see me, I get no comfort to my soul by any second means under heaven but from those who are nicknamed Puritans. They are the men that can give a word of comfort to a wearied soul in due season, and that I have found by experience . . .

THE LAST AND HEAVENLY SPEECHES, AND
GLORIOUS DEPARTURE, OF JOHN, VISCOUNT KENMURE

AM I
A CHRISTIAN?

James Fraser of Brea

Taken from
'Memoirs of the Rev. James Fraser of Brea',
in *Scottish Puritans—Select Biographies*, Vol. 2

THE BANNER OF TRUTH TRUST

THE BANNER OF TRUTH TRUST
3 Murrayfield Road, Edinburgh EH12 6EL, UK
P.O. Box 621, Carlisle, PA 17013, USA

*

© The Banner of Truth Trust 2009

ISBN-13: 978 1 84871 014 6

*

Typeset in 10.5 / 13.5 pt Adobe Caslon Pro
at the Banner of Truth Trust, Edinburgh

Printed in the USA by
Versa Press, Inc.,
East Peoria, IL

*

Only minor editorial adjustments have been made
to the original text, e.g. the modernizing of some
words and the supply of Scripture references.

AM I
A CHRISTIAN?

*Declaring the objective grounds of my
doubting my conversion and actual
interest in Christ, with the special
and general answers thereto.*

Since the time I knew any thing of God until this day, the tempter has not ceased to make me continually raze the foundations. And I find that it has been his first and greatest object to make me doubt of my conversion, by proposing false marks, and making me to imagine grace to be another thing than indeed it was; and by inconsiderate reading of marks of sanctification given in good books, some of which I found afterwards not well cautioned, and by a confident asserting I was not converted. So that, for the space of three years after my real conversion, I not only doubted of my conversion, but believed that I was all the time rather in an unconverted state, but thought I was in the way and had good hopes.

But the Lord making the fruits of sanctification to appear, I began to think otherwise, and in process of time to think rather I was converted, and to settle that as a conclusion, which, though the devil cannot totally overturn, yet ceases he not to shake it, which by search I found out to be summed up in these twenty branches.

Ground 1.

Because there was not such a distinct, long, orderly, and deep work of preparation and humiliation at first conversion as I found described in practical books writing of the new birth.

Answer

There was a work of the almighty power of Christ discovering sin and a natural condition as the greatest evils, which put me out to restless endeavours to come out of this; and I found the inability of myself and all duties to bring me out of this condition. And the Lord did by a marvellous light discover the Lord Jesus to me as the Saviour of sinners and their full happiness; and my heart immediately closed with him wholly and fully, which in its fruits has continued to this day.

Secondly, that though the substantials of conversion be observed generally amongst all, yet do not all persons' cases agree as to the circumstantials of conversion, that is, as to the length, measure, and manner of the spirit of bondage, as is likewise clear from Scripture.

Thirdly, the question is not so much how Christ came in, as if he be in. If you find the fruits of holiness, it is well, though you know not how they were sown or grown; 'The kingdom of heaven cometh not with observation' (*Luke* 17:20).

GROUND 2.

My ordinary, uneven, unsettled, unprof-
itable way of walking with the Lord, the
ordinary strayings and departings of my heart
from God; which unstableness in all my ways
makes me fear double-mindedness, and to
question whether my heart did ever find and
see the exceeding evil of sin, seeing I so easily
fall into it; and how this can consist with the
love of God that ought to be in the heart.

ANSWER

Though I cannot deny these sins as to
the matter, yet these considerations are sug-
gested unto me as answer thereunto:

(1.) They are not the spots of the world
(*2 Pet.* 2:13); they are as to their nature like

the 'spots of his children', they are unwatch-fulness, shortcomings as to the heights of duty, idle words, fits of unbelief, carnality in the use of lawful comforts.

(2.) I bless God they are not the sins of the time; I have been through grace kept from bowing of the knee to Baal. If I die in this wilderness, it is for my own sin, and not that I have any part in the general con-spiracy.

(3.) I find they interrupt not the Lord's kindness utterly, but find that in my worst his 'visitations uphold my spirit'.

(4.) Though the bush be burning, yet it is not consumed; the spark of spiritual life that the Lord has kindled remains still burning, yea, and increasing, for all these showers of sin that seek to quench it.

(5.) Though I have departed, yet not wickedly from God. I sin neither deliberately, delightfully, with full consent, nor lie impenitently in my sins; I grieve and mourn for them, and hate them.

(6.) I find sin on the decaying hand.

(7.) I find advantages by my sins: *peccare nocet, peccavisse vero juvat.*[1] I may say, as Mr Fox, my sins have in a manner done me more good than my graces. Grace and mercy 'hath abounded where sin hath abounded'. I am made more humble, watchful, revengeful against myself, to see a greater need to

---

[1] 'To sin harms, to have sinned truly helps.'

depend more upon him, to love him the more that continues such kindness to me notwithstanding of my manifold provocations. I find that true which Shepard said, 'Sin loses strength by every new fall.'

Ground 3.

My fearful, dark, hellish ignorance, and carnal conceptions of God, heaven, and hell, by which I am tempted to draw this conclusion, that I am yet in darkness, and that that marvellous light which discovers Christ really as he is; the glory of the Father, has not shined on my soul; but that all my knowledge is either rational, or notional, or natural. Oh my unspeakable ignorance of him!

Answer

To which, for satisfaction, I answer these things:

(1.) That no man has seen God face to face, but in his back parts, which is a very imperfect knowledge (*Exod.* 33:23); this was it that Moses saw.

(2.) Saints 'see but through a glass', not immediately in this life (*1 Cor.* 13:12).

(3.) And hence they see but darkly, as in a mystery (*1 Cor.* 13:12).

(4.) The most eminent saints have much lamented their ignorance of God, 'I am more brutish than any man, and have not the understanding of the holy' (*Prov.* 30:2). O how little a portion of him is known!

(5.) This is a time of absence, and it is but a dark knowledge we have of one not present; it is in heaven we will 'see face to face, and know as we are known, and see Christ as he is' (*1 John* 3:3).

(6.) 'We walk by faith, and not by sight' (*2 Cor.* 5:7). Seeing is our life in heaven, not here. It is a controversy whether the sight we have here of Christ be specifically different from what they have in heaven.

(7.) It is worth considering that when Job saw the Lord extraordinarily, he thought his former knowledge but a knowing God by the hearing of the ear (*Job* 42:5); and yet, when Job knew but by the hearing of the ear, and not by the seeing of the eye, he was then a 'just man, that feared God, and eschewed evil' (*Job* 1:1).

(8.) I saw the Lord in glory with the eyes of my mind once extraordinarily, and as I thought intuitively, the impression and effects of which remain to this day.

(9.) I have and find the real effects of saving knowledge. I trust in him, 'They that know thy name will put their trust in thee' (*Psa.* 9:10). It makes me prize and esteem him, and long for him above all things, and mourn for his absence as the greatest evil, 'If thou knewest the gift of God, and who it is that asketh water of thee, thou wouldest ask' (*John* 4:10). Though the thing be not seen in its cause, yet it is seen in its effects.

(10.) Folk may really see and know God, though they neither mind it nor know it, yea, though they think they do not so, Philip desired to see the Father, as though he had never been revealed to him; and yet

Christ tells him he saw him, because he saw Christ (*John* 14:9).

(11.) The Lord says, 'To execute judgment is to know the Lord.' Our knowledge of God is better discovered in our obedience to him than in our uptakings of him.

(12.) As 'herein is love, not that we loved God, but that he loved us', so herein is knowledge, not that we know him, but rather, as the apostle says, 'are known of him' (*Gal.* 4:9). What shall I say, lastly, but as Mr Shepard on the subject, 'If ever the Lord has revealed Christ to you, you will go mourning to the grave for want of him, and for your ignorance of him so long.' The Lord knows that it is the thing in the world I have most desired—to know God and to see his glory.

Ground 4.

That seldom has there been a glorious, clear, distinct, and full covenanting with God. Something I remember of the Lord's wooing of me; and how can the Lord be mine unless some marriage-day has been? And whenever I have gone about this duty, how much heartlessness and confusion? In trouble I have been, but not a distinct delivery.

Answer

This objection is of the same nature with the first, and therefore I answer:

(1.) When the Lord first made me see a need of himself, and my misery in the want of him, and had wearied me of myself, I remember then he discovered the Lord Jesus in his loveliness, and my soul, even my whole soul, was made fully and for evermore to close with him, and him only, and above all, and for all things. And as this was the upshot of my tossings, so was it the seed of all good that ever followed, and I was made to express this much.

(2.) As, in the preparatory work of humiliation, the Lord observes not the same method with all, so in the soul's closing with Christ, all do it not under the same distinct notion. Some do it explicitly, and expressly subscribe with heart and hand that they are the Lord's, and swear loyalty to him; some close with Christ implicitly and really, their heart clinging to him and his ways, though they be not distinct and express in this; yea, some close with Christ, and are married to him by and under the notion of believing on him with all their heart for all things, and so cast themselves on Christ; and this is covenanting, as covenanting is believing. And therefore is faith expressed under several notions and terms, according to the variety of men's apprehensions of it, and the several exercises of the soul in going out after and closing with Christ. Believing on Christ, and the will's liking of Christ, and personal covenanting with Christ, are all one upon the matter, namely, the soul's union with Christ; the Lord is yours, however, and you are his. It is both a private and public solemn marriage; if once you know any thing of it, look not for solemn marriages every day. Hardly is the renewal of a covenant, which is frequent, so glorious and signal as the first marriage-day.

GROUND 5.

Not only the dim apprehensions, but the unkindly uptakings and conceivings of the Lord in Christ, as a strange God, and not under the kindly relation of a father, and friend, and husband, which breeds aversion to him, so as I cannot trust on him with my whole heart. And this makes me fear I am but under the relation of a servant, wanting the Spirit of adoption, and that I am yet but a stranger, and not drawn near to him in Christ, not a son.

ANSWER

To which I answer these things:

(1.) That however in the beginning there was ground for this complaint, yet that now there is no such cause, because that by serious meditation on Christ, on his offices, on his attitude towards sinners, and on his works of providence towards myself, both as to my spiritual and temporal condition, I have been helped to see the Lord, and take him up under the kindly notion of a father, yea, of my best and nearest friend, of my life, hope, health, and light, so as 'I am a stranger on earth' with God.

(2.) That though many are sons indeed, and 'have not received the spirit of bondage again to fear', yet do they take to themselves this spirit again; and the Lord suffers this, that even his children be as servants, especially in the beginning, though they be lords of all; and that the bond-woman with her son remain with the heir of the promise (*Gal.* 4:1-2, 24).

(3.) That as no sin is perfectly healed in this life, so neither is the legal spirit of fear perfectly cast out; but when love is perfect, it will east out fear (*1 John* 4:18), and is daily casting it out.

(4.) That as it is in children who know not distinctly their parents, but as strangers are afraid of them, yet have a secret instinct of nature, their heart warms, and cannot be kept away from them; so I have found with myself, when most under bondage and hardest apprehensions of God, that yet some kind of correspondence has been kept up, and that I have mourned for his absence as under the greatest evil, could not be kept from him, was intimate and homely, though I had not such boldness and confidence to be heard.

Ground 6.

Because I am tempted to think I have not been visited with special love, or the favour the Lord shows to his people; and that all my enlargements, visitations, light, change of heart, are but common mercies, no extraordinary thing. And what can I build on them?

Answer

I answer:

(1.) That though at first there appear little more than common mercies in them, yet have I, by a more narrow search, found some special love and favour engraven upon them, as I purpose to show afterwards.

(2.) What we meet with now are but the earnest of the bargain,[2] and that is little in respect of the bargain itself; and it matters not whether the earnest be little or much (2 *Cor.* 5:5).

(3.) We should judge of the Lord's love rather by his sanctifying influences, humbling and strengthening the heart, than by his ravishing enjoyments and consolations: we see the dreadful end of such as boast much of that; it is the 'adulterous generation' that 'seeks after' such 'signs' (*Matt.* 12:39).

(4.) The way and manner of conveyance of mercies and spiritual visitations are

---

[2] the earnest of the bargain: the deposit or first instalment that guarantees the full payment.

rather to be looked to than themselves. See if you have them by prayer, if you have them of free grace, if they represent, hold out, and draw to God; and the Lord be stamped on them; not the gift but the giver: this day of small things is not to be despised.

(5.) The people of God are a poor and needy people, kept empty, have all their fulness in Christ, in the promise; and is to be revealed in heaven, where their treasure is.

(6.) This is an evil time, a time of famine and beggary, in which it is good to be preserved from starving, and in which a little is worth twice as much at another time.[3]

---

[3] This was written in a time of persecution, when spiritual as well as material food was in short supply.

Ground 7.

That the mercies received come not in a gracious way, not as the answer of prayers, or as the result of my patient waiting, but as it were by chance, my mercies often meeting with my worst frame.

Answer

To which I answer:

(1.) I have prayed, mourned, waited, and hoped for mercies, though with much weakness and imperfection. It is not the degree but the nature that is to be looked to.

(2.) They are not the fruits of my prayers and endeavours; for there is more ground of loathing me for these than rewarding me. But they are come in a better and more comfortable way, namely, by grace. The Lord matches mercies with our indispositions, that grace may be seen. It is rather a sign of love than hatred, that grace is stamped on all favours and enjoyments; 'Not unto us, but unto thy name' (*Psa.* 115:1). It is better to hold mercies by this title. It is not fit that the Lord's love should be proportioned to our endeavours; where were grace then? 'Not of works, lest any man should boast' (*Eph.* 2:9).

(3.) They draw to God.

GROUND 8.

The Lord behaves as a stranger and an enemy to me, crossing me in all my ways, not giving me my will, so that it would seem he were not my father.

ANSWER

To this I answer these things:

(1.) That he causes grief, and shows wrath, yet not pure wrath; he 'takes not his loving-kindnesses utterly away' (cf. *Psa.* 89:33), but they are 'renewed every morning' (cf. *Lam.* 3:23). He shows much kindness in the midst of all his judgments.

(2.) Our will, like children, is not our well; and it is a mercy to be crossed in this. God knows what is best for us.

(3.) This is a time of wrath, a night; and what wonder if storms and darkness be?

(4.) You see, saints have complained of this: 'Why art thou unto me as an enemy?' Job says, 'Thou art cruel unto me' (cf. *Job* 33:10; 30:21).

(5.) Feelings represent God falsely; it is to feelings and imaginations that God thus appears, not to faith. We should take other interpreters than feelings.

(6.) We should not look upon all things that may be trials as effects of wrath: 'God hideth man from his purpose' (cf. *Job.* 33:17), that he may hide pride, that the soul may be patient and humble, and exercise faith.

(7.) It is utterly wrong that anything outside of us should make us doubt our inward sincerity, seeing these are extrinsic to it: 'No man knoweth love or hatred by anything under the sun' (cf. *Eccles.* 9:1).

Ground 9.

That prayers are not directly and plainly answered.

Answer

To this I answer:

(1.) As in the former, that it is a thing outside of us, and so extrinsic to our sincerity. In this matter, regard is to be had rather to the manner of our prayers than to our answers.

(2.) There is no fear, if you pray in the name of Christ, in faith, in humility, and sincerity, though they should not be answered.

(3.) I have ever been helped in my extremity, in the deep (*Psa.* 130:1).

(4.) It is an ordinary complaint of saints (*Psa.* 22:1-2; *Lam.* 3:8), 'He shutteth out my prayer.'

(5.) Prayers may be suspended when they are not rejected (*Luke* 18:4, 7).

(6.) There is no fear while you continue in well-doing; for 'in due time ye shall reap, if ye faint not' (*Gal.* 6:9). Where God has given a mouth and stomach, he will give meat. Your cause is in dependence, not overthrown; and it is good that you get what will bear your expenses till a decision be given.

(7.) I find myself better and worse as I increase or decay in prayer; a token they are not altogether in vain.

(8.) Prayers may be heard, and you not know it (*Hos.* 11:3).

(9.) The answer of prayers is not ordinarily direct and plain in the terms of our petition, but indirect; you have not the same thing you seek, but you are answered equivalently in as good.

(10.) I get promises renewed.

(11.) It is like, when the Lord will build up Zion, there will be many answers dispatched. Now is a sowing time; hereafter is our harvest, and then all petitions shall be answered.

(12.) After search, I found some petitions directly answered; and it is want of taking up and considering our returns, or our own sloth, that hinders us from discerning our returns. Sometimes the Lord hears, and we are so prejudiced that we will not believe it, as in Job's case.

Ground 10.

Lack of compassion for, and deep apprehension of, the lamentable soul's case of my unconverted relations and ignorant, profane, formal, neighbours: oh it lies not heavy on my spirit! Do I believe therefore a hell or heaven, or that the ignorant or unconverted shall go to hell?

Answer

I answer:

(1.) By confessing that there is great want of compassion, and faith, and seriousness in this, and that there is great deadness—Lord help it; for we believe, love, and prophesy but in part only.

(2.) I mourn for this, and this deadness is loathsome and hateful to me.

(3.) I am yet helped, upon occasional views of their condition, to have my sorrow stirred, and to be earnest for them with the Lord, yea, and to pour forth tears and sighs of grief for them, and to find my compassion sensibly stirred.

GROUND 11.

There is a constant indisposition of spirit to all manner of duties, unwillingness to enter to them, wearied and heartless in them, and glad when they are done; so that I fear there is not a new nature which delights in the law of God.

ANSWER

To which I answer these things:

(1.) That as there is a regenerate and unregenerate part in every believer, which is continually opposite to that which is good; so this indisposition proceeds from the unregenerate part, in which no good thing dwells (*Rom.* 7:18); and this should make us question our state no more than the being of a body of death.

(2.) That I find something in me that mourns under this, which esteems, approves, and sees a glory and delight in the law of the Lord (*Rom.* 7:22). 'The spirit is willing, but the flesh is weak' (*Matt.* 26:41).

(3.) That therefore I am not so much wearied of the duty, (which I love) but of my own ill heart in the duty: as a loving son, that has a pained foot, is willing to run his father's errand, and glad to be employed, and yet the sore foot makes the journey a burden; there is a thorn in the flesh. An unsound heart's opposition is to the duty itself; hypocrites love not all duties.

Ground 12.

Because I found not a full resolution to obey some difficult commands, such as plain and free reproof, especially of great folk; plain dealing with my acquaintances as to their state: which makes me think I am not universal as to my obedience; and that I am but partial in my obedience.

Answer

To this I answer these things:

(1.) That though I exceedingly fail in the manner as being heartless, general, and having base ends, not altogether respecting the good of the party I deal with; yet, through grace, I win to do the duty as to the matter and substance of it.

(2.) That when I do it, I find I do it not only to ease my conscience, but out of respect to the command of God.

(3.) That I prize, love, esteem, and have respect to this duty, and my heart would be at it; and am straitened and in pain till I discharge it. I approve that 'the law is holy' (*Rom.* 7:12).

(4.) I pray, mourn, and loathe myself under my failings in this, and have fetched it to Christ; and it is strange to me that that sin, for which I groan to the Lord Jesus to be delivered from it, should or can damn me. It is the Lord's controversy: 'Wilt thou not be made clean?'

(5.) It is through accident that those duties are omitted, through my natural bashful temper. A man would do a thing willingly, but is in bonds that he cannot get it done; I find that 'when I would do good, evil is present' (*Rom.* 7:21).

(6.) There is not a full conviction of the duty, but especially of the way and manner how it should be performed; 'How to do I know not' (cf. *Rom.* 7:18).

Ground 13.

That I am not so taken up in heart with heaven, in longing after it, delighting and rejoicing in the expectations thereof; and, therefore, my heart not being there, it is likely it is not my treasure.

Answer

To which I answer:

(1.) Look, as when Philip said to Christ, 'Show us the Father, and it sufficeth us'; Christ answers, 'You have known him, because he that hath seen me hath seen the Father' (*John* 14:8-9): so I say, he that desires and mourns after Christ mourns for sin, and desires to be holy, loves the fellowship of God's people, really does love and long for heaven; for what is heaven but the enjoyment of Christ and conformity to him, though in a more clear and distinct notion?

(2.) My unwillingness to go to heaven proceeds from a desire to do some service for Christ before I go: much of my work I suspect is yet undone.

(3.) This proceeded from a want of a full assurance of my future happiness and some fears; for I love the thing.

(4.) I find myself of late more distinct and clear in my longings after, and joyful expectations of heaven, and my heart more heavenly-minded.

Ground 14.

That I grow not, nor have success; nor am I going through with my work, but ever after one manner.

Answer

I answer:

(1.) That though there may be growth in grace, yet it appears not always sensibly, but grows as a seed of corn, and a man knows not; it 'comes not with observation' (*Luke* 17:20).

(2.) Notwithstanding of remaining evils, yet do I find a remarkable growth, though not in the bulk of graces, yet as to the nature and purity; I have made better work, though not so much of it; I work more evangelically than I did before, with purer ends; I grow downward if not upward.

(3.) I have found a growth in faith, in love, in patience, in humility; dying to the world and myself and self-righteousness, and living unto God: though in that which I propose to myself there is no growth. Yea—,

(4.) There is an expediency, if not a necessity, of pulling down a certain kind of righteousness; and hence a man shall find himself worse than before, before ever the righteousness of God be set up.

Ground 15.

Because I find such an evil heart in me,
such blindness, hardness of heart, carnality,
pride, and other sins, and in such an high
degree, that I say, Did ever the Lord renew
this heart?

Answer

I answer:

(1.) 'In me, that is, in my flesh, dwelleth
no good thing' (*Rom.* 7:18); and as to my
unrenewed part, I am 'carnal, and sold
under sin' (*Rom.* 7:14). There is a 'body of
death' in all (*Rom.* 7:24).

(2.) As I find this in my flesh, so do I
find a new man, that knows, delights in the

Lord and his ways, and continually hates and opposes the body of death.

GROUND 16.

That I enjoy not this Lord himself in ordinances, in public or private prayer, in hearing of the word, or reading thereof, or through meditation. There is not that special fellowship with the Lord himself, nor the glory or power of Christ found and seen; some light and strength, but little or none of God.

ANSWER

To this I answer:

(1.) That I really desire and love the Lord Christ above any thing, and mourn for want of him, and come to ordinances for himself, and am unsatisfied with any thing, though never so glorious, if it fetch not nor reveal a Christ to me. Yea, I love every thing for his cause mostly; and it makes every mercy sweet to me, that it comes from the Lord.

(2.) Although through mine own sloth and unbelief, and because of an evil time and day of wrath, there are not such plain and full visions of God; yet have I found ordinances, and duties, and works of providence, reveal something of the Lord himself, and of his love and greatness, so as my soul has been drawn to the Lord himself thereby, and to love, and admire, and adore, and delight in him the more.

(3.) I have found the ordinances and means (though not sensibly nor presently, yet) in process of time bringing forth real fruits of holiness, so as I had reason to bless the Lord for such occasions; even as my body is really (though not sensibly) nourished by meat and drink. However, this point deserves a more serious consideration.

Ground 17.

That my thoughts of sin, of hell, and of heaven, do not beget such lively impressions upon my soul. I tremble not at sin, death, and hell; I am not rejoicing in hope of glory; and this makes me think my knowledge and faith is but dead and lifeless.

Answer

To this I answer:

(1.) That though in my sensitive faculty I find not these impressions of joy and fear, yet do I find them in my estimative, appreciative faculty; so as I really judge sin to be the greatest evil, and am really most troubled with it; and I judge Christ, his grace and holiness, to be really the greatest good. A man is more pained, tormented, troubled, and cries out more for a boil on his finger than he does when he knows he has a hectic fever or consumption; and yet he truly judges the one a greater evil than the other. There is more fear and grief in the damned for sin than in any saint; and a soul newly converted and drawn to the ways of God, with assurance of Christ's love, has more sensible joy than a grown, assured Christian. Grace goes not by the sensible impressions on the affections, or rising of the sensitive faculty or appetite, which outward and sensible objects do elevate.

(2.) Saints have found and lamented this distemper, as it is such, and yet have not quit their interest, 'Why hast thou hardened our hearts from thy fear?' (*Isa.* 63:17). And hence David and the church do cry frequently for quickening, 'Quicken us, O Lord, and we will call on thy name' (*Psa.* 80:18).

(3.) Baxter says well, 'Hardness of heart is more in the will and practice than in the sensitive faculty'; as is easy proven by Scripture. Disobedience is hardness of heart in Scripture.

GROUND 18.

This is from my spiritual pride, which streams itself through all my actions, even my most spiritual: and hence I find that I resolve to be holy, to get an esteem, not from men but from conscience; I mourn for sin as it is a weakness, and as it is contrary to my design and resolutions. Yea, though I find an insufficiency in duties to save me, and so of necessity made to flee to another, yet do I find my heart secretly wishing that it were otherwise, that life were to be had through our own works; and this makes me secretly desire and endeavour to do something on earth that might be a part of my crown in heaven: and I found a despising of the glory revealed in heaven, if freely given, and no way merited; so that I am by this put to question whether ever I was dead to the law or not.

ANSWER

To which I answer, omitting what may be answered to this by what has been said, I satisfy myself with this, that as I find a spirit of self and pride acting, so do I find a spirit of humility loathing myself for this my pride, and a secret contentedness in breaking my resolutions even when they were good, because self was thereby debased, and the counsel of the Lord did stand: yea, and I find 'I rejoice in my infirmities, that the power of Christ may rest upon me' (2 Cor. 12:9); and I love heaven the better, because it is the purchase of Christ's blood, and the fruit of free grace.

Secondly, 'Self will be in every action (says Shepard) and this body of death will discover itself thus, as well as any other way.'

GROUND 19.

I find such instability in my heart and ways, such unequal steps between the Lord and my idols, that I fear my whole heart is not come to the Lord; I am not his only. Oh the one heart, the united heart, the conjugal heart! But, alas! mine is parted between the Lord and idols; and I sometimes delight in the Lord, and sometimes in my idols and worldly contentment, they served the Lord, and they served their idols. (2 Kings 17:33).

ANSWER

I answer:

(1.) No man ever closed so fully with Christ, or had such a conjugal love, but had some inclinations to idols, by reason of the unregenerate part. Our union of faith and love is imperfect, as well as any other grace; the unregenerate carnal part cries still for, and would be at, its lovers. In heaven our affections shall be wholly for the Lord.

(2.) The renewed part is for the Lord wholly and only, and gives not consent to what the flesh does, but is led captive, and sighs under the bondage, and cries out against its own heart-whorishness, and the denomination is taken from the better part. 'O miserable man that I am, who shall deliver me from this body of death?' (*Rom.* 7:24). Unrenewed men contentedly and allowedly divide their affections, they loathe not nor abhor themselves.

(3.) I find the Lord's interest growing stronger and stronger in my soul.

GROUND 20.

*When I read that the 'unprofitable serv-
ant is cast into utter darkness', and consider the
great disproportion that is between my service
and my rule and the former practice of saints,
I cannot conceive how I can go to heaven,
how the just Lord will give heaven to such an
unprofitable servant; will ever Christ say to
me, 'Well done, good and faithful servant'?*

ANSWER

But for this I answer these things:

(1.) Heaven is not promised to the
degree or measure of grace, but to the
nature of it; the Lord accepts mites, cups
of cold water, grains of mustard-seed; he

will not quench smoking flax: I do service, though I cannot weigh it in measure.

(2.) Such is the condescendency and lovely nature of Christ, that he will crown those duties we are ashamed to own. Christ counts and prizes saints' duties more than any thing else in the world: 'Ye visited me, fed me, gave me drink. When saw we thee hungry or naked? In that ye did it to one of these little ones, ye did it to me' (*Matt.* 25:35 ff.). It is Christ's gracious property, he is soon pleased, and his yoke is easy. Parents are wonderfully taken up with the poorest and simplest action or speeches of their children. There is a fatherly love in Christ.

(3.) Heaven comes by grace, by Christ's blood, and not by works; works are not your

title to glory. 'No law music', says Rutherford, 'in heaven'; no, 'worthy is the Lamb.'
Look not to what you have done, but to
what Christ has done; you neither share in
whole nor in part with Christ: good works
are mentioned, not to buy or purchase glory
by, but to evidence an interest in Christ and
sincerity in grace; if there be as much as will
evidence sincerity, there is enough. The least
gold is gold as well as the greatest piece.

JAMES FRASER
AND CONVERSION[1]

My old and honoured friend Dr Elder
Cumming of Glasgow, in his admir-
able appreciation of Fraser expresses his
regret that Fraser so often uses the word
'conversion' concerning his whole Christian
life. But after giving the fullest consideration to what that deeply experienced and
deservedly eminent evangelical preacher says
concerning Fraser's frequent use of the word

[1] From an article by Alexander Whyte (1836-1921).

'conversion', I cannot share with him in that criticism and complaint of his. For so far as I understand Fraser he employs that experimental and autobiographical word in much the same sense in which your Lord employs it when he is instructing his disciples concerning the inwardness and the depth and the intricacy and the unceasing progress of the spiritual life in their souls.

Our Lord must have startled his already converted disciples, and he must have made the dullest-minded of them to ponder and to think, when, seeing their pride and their ambition and their jealousy and their envy of one another, he called a little child unto him, and said to them, 'Except ye be converted, and become as the little child, ye shall not enter into the kingdom of heaven.' And after Peter had been three years called and converted and had been all that time under the continual tuition of his Master, warning that proud disciple of his coming fall, his Master said to him, 'When thou art converted from thy coming fall and art truly penitent for it and art forgiven it, then strengthen thy brethren in all their similar trials and temptations and falls.'

Now it is in that experimental and autobiographical and vivid sense that James Fraser employs this word 'conversion' so often concerning himself. And it is in that same experimental sense that I shall now employ it when I proceed to speak to you for a little concerning Fraser and concerning yourselves.

'A Christian man's whole life', says our author in his fifth chapter, 'is but a continual conversion. And the Lord after every time of backsliding draws our souls back again to himself very much in the same way as at our first conversion. Yea, he deals with us sometimes as if we had never been converted before.'

'For myself', he says, 'I have found a far deeper and a far more distinct law-work in my after convictions of sin than ever I felt at my first conviction. I was converted that communion week in Edinburgh as with a clap. But now the Lord draws me back and back to himself, step by step, so that I am better and better prepared for Christ before every time of my renewed returns to him.'

Do you follow that, my friends? Do you take Fraser up? You have had that same experience yourselves, have you not? Your law-work, as Paul experienced it and then wrote to the Romans about it, and as Fraser experienced it and now writes to you about it, your own law-work is a thousand times more deep and deadly in your after life than ever it was or could be at your first conviction and conversion. With most converts in their first experiences their law-work is but skin deep, so to speak. But the awful spirituality of God's holy law is all experienced more and more as the soul attains to a true spirituality itself.

As Fraser says, 'It is only after we have come to know Christ better, and better, and ever better; it is only then that we come back to him with more and more conviction of our utter and everlasting hopelessness but for him, and but for his all-sufficient salvation.' Just so. No young convert, the very best, as yet knows much of himself. Paul did not. Luther, our second Paul, did not. Fraser, our second Luther, did not. No man ever did at first. The unsounded depth of our own depravity, the bottomless pit of sin and misery that is in us all—that takes a long lifetime for its full discovery. Indeed it is never fully discovered to us in this life— else we would go mad at the sight of it. The Holy Spirit has many awful things to show his subjects about themselves, but they are not able to bear all those awful things as yet; no more than a little child is able to bear all that lies wrapped up in its own soul against its threescore and ten years to come.

'But now', says the minister of Culross as he began to grow toward his threescore and ten years in the spiritual life, 'but now the Lord insists on my seeing every step of my returns to him. So that all the early knowledge I had of myself and of him now seems to me to be as no knowledge at all compared with what I have now.'

Again, and further on in my pursuit of this intricate man, I find this: 'The whole subsequent life of a truly Christian man is one continual conversion, in which he is perpetually humbled under an awful and an unbearable sense of his own incurable sinfulness.' That is to say, he is perpetually cast down in his own soul; he is perpetually degraded in his own eyes; he is perpetually disgusted at himself; he is perpetually horrified at himself.

In reading Sir John Coleridge's beautiful biography of John Keble the other day I came on an exact case of this same experience. John Keble was perpetually humbled under his own inward and unconquerable sinfulness, till he could not keep his humiliation out of his *Christian Year,* nor out of his private letters to such intimate friends as his future biographer. But Sir John cannot comprehend Keble. He had never had that perpetual humiliation himself, and able and good man as Sir John was, his shamefaced apologies for his friend and his exculpatory explanations of his too strong language all make me smile at his babe-like innocence.

I wonder what Sir John would have said about James Fraser if Dean Ramsay, or some other of his Edinburgh correspondents, had been bold enough to send him a birthday gift of our intricate and perpetually humbled autobiography. Alexander the Great always had his camp-bed made with Homer under his pillow because of the incomparable battle-pieces in that book of battles. And Keble would have somehow found out James Fraser, and would have kept him under his pillow, had the Laird of Brea been in the Church of England, or been in the Church of Rome. But Scotland was 'Samaria' to Keble and to all the other Tractarians of those days. All the same, I know more than one old convert in Scotland who read that intricate book with their midnight lamp, and who find a true companionship in such frequent passages as these:

'I am perpetually humbled under the experience of my own sinfulness; till I creep nearer and nearer to God in Christ, and with more and more fervent faith and love every day and every night. And till I am drawn continually to walk closer and closer with Christ, endeavouring after his likeness in all my walk and conversation.'

In spite of Sir John Coleridge, and all such innocent and easily sanctified men, the Laird of Brea keeps on returning and returning to his deadly need of a more and more radical and more and more root-and-branch conversion all his days. He says:

I have been searching into the Lord's ends with all this in my case. And I have come to this conclusion in this matter. I think he has taken these ways with me so that I might know something of the unspeakable plague of my own heart, and that I might be more and more humbled because of my continual departing from God. Also this I think has been one of his ends with me: that I might be the better acquainted with his various processes and methods and his different styles of conversion, with which through my own somewhat hasty incoming I was not at that time so well acquainted. God does now, as it were, act my conversion over and over again. He convinces me more and more, not only of my actual and my open sins, but still more now of my secret and my soul-sins, of the plague of my own heart, and of that fountain-sin of my very nature, which carries me away from my God and from his holiness continually. He convinces me also that this is a matter in which I cannot really help myself, or redeem myself, or in any way cure myself, do all I can. And all that, till I am shut up to believe, and to trust, and to live in and on Christ as never before. And then in all that, that I might be the better able to guide and to direct such of his people as he is pleased to put under my charge at Culross or else where.

Now, speaking of Culross, what do you think? For my part, I cannot but think that it was by far their greatest blessing in this world to have the Laird of Brea for their parish minister—that so difficult to convert and so intricate-minded man. And I think I know some of yourselves who would willingly have walked across the whole peninsula of Fife to have spent the weekend at Culross. We are told that Ezra the scribe stood upon a pulpit of wood which the carpenters of Jerusalem had made for the purpose, and he read in the Book of the Law distinctly, and gave the sense, and made the people to understand the reading. And exactly like that was the Laird of Brea in his pulpit of wood at Culross. He made his parishioners to understand the law of God through the law-work that was first in their minister's own heart, and then through all that in their own hearts. So much so, that all the people in that favoured parish who were already converted, and all those who collected into the parish kirk every Sabbath-day seeking conversion, would almost worship James Fraser as the people of Anwoth were already almost worshipping Samuel Rutherford.

For on every returning Sabbath-day Fraser went up into his pulpit of wood and gave out such psalms and such paraphrases and selected such Scriptures and so drew out their deepest sense as to throw a divine light on the hearts of all his spiritually-minded people; till, like his favourite divine Thomas Shepard of New England, Fraser would never have a Sabbath on which both he and his like-minded kirk-session did not expect some young converts to be added to the church, and some old backsliders to be restored to it.

Now, may this pulpit of wood in which I now stand be like the pulpit of Ezra in Jerusalem and like the pulpit of Fraser in Culross! And may I and my colleague be your Ezra and your Fraser? And all that first to our own true and intricate and repeated and completed conversion! And then to the same completed conversion in you all! And all to the glory of God both in us and in you! Amen.

JAMES FRASER OF BREA

A BRIEF SKETCH OF HIS LIFE

James Fraser was born on his father's estate at Brea, in the parish of Resolis, Black Isle, Ross-shire, on July 29, 1639. His father, Sir James Fraser, a knight and brother of Lord Lovat, sat in the Glasgow Assembly of 1638 which along with other revolutionary measures, abolished and outlawed prelacy in Scotland.

The estate which the young James inherited in his minority long remained a source of legal and financial difficulties.

After gaining his M.A. in 1658 at Marischal College, Aberdeen, he turned to law. At this point in his life he was not long converted and did not consider himself free to prepare for the Christian ministry due to his legal entanglements and his conscientious objection to the new Episcopalian Church regime. After briefly considering the principles of the Quakers, he began to teach Scripture and was ordained in 1670 or 1672 by some ejected ministers.

During this period he preached frequently without being arrested. In July 1674 he was summoned to appear before the Privy Council and, when he refused, was denounced as a rebel. His eventual arrest came in 1677 and, through the strenuous efforts of James Sharp, was imprisoned on the notorious Bass Rock.

Alexander Smellie writes that 'no persecution could make his heart bankrupt or could lessen his fruit-bearing. "Every day", he [Fraser] records, "I read the Scriptures, exhorted and taught therefrom, did sing psalms, and prayed with such of our society as our masters did permit to worship God together, and this two times a day. I studied Hebrew and Greek, and gained some knowledge in these Oriental languages. I likewise read some divinity, and wrote a Treatise on Faith, with some other miscellanies, and letters to Christian friends and relations." He could scarcely have done more if he had been at home in his northern manse.'

Fraser was set free in 1679 in the general indulgence given to all Nonconformists who had taken no part in the rising at

Bothwell Bridge. However, he was arrested again in 1681, and this time confined to Blackness Castle in West Lothian. Six weeks later he was released, but was forced into exile. After preaching and yet another imprisonment, this time in London, he returned to Scotland in 1687. Following the Glorious Revolution of 1688-9 he first preached at a meetinghouse in Culross, a town on the north-western shores of the Firth of Forth, before later becoming parish minister there until his death in 1698.

Fraser is chiefly remembered for his *Memoirs*, which were first published in Edinburgh in 1738, and which have been reprinted by the Banner of Truth Trust in *Scottish Puritans—Select Biographies*, Vol. 2. The *Memoirs* are a record of the Lord's dealings with him in the course of his 'pilgrimage'. Speaking about Fraser's *Memoirs* Alexander Whyte said that Fraser 'will live as long as a scholarly religion, and an evangelical religion, and a spiritual religion, and a profoundly experimental religion lives in his native land'. As a searching spiritual autobiography, the *Memoirs* have, according to Whyte, 'few, if any equals' (*James Fraser, Laird of Brea*, Edinburgh: Oliphant, Anderson and Ferrier, 1911, p. 3).

OTHER BOOKS IN THE
POCKET PURITANS
SERIES

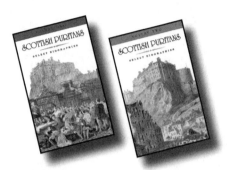

The 17th century was a dynamic period in Scottish church history, and yet many of its rich records lay hidden in privately owned manuscripts for two hundred years. It was only with the evangelical awakening of the 1840s that close attention was given to their publication, and a Society, formed for that purpose in Edinburgh, took the name of the historian, Robert Wodrow (1679-1734). On the 26 volumes thus published subsequent authors have depended heavily, and particularly so with respect to the two volumes originally entitled *Select Biographies*. In an era when Puritan literature is again being rediscovered their reprint is timely, providing as it does the opportunity to go back to first-hand sources. Here, for the most part, men and women live in their own words, or in the witness of their contemporaries. The 19th-century editor, William Tweedie, himself an evangelical leader, thought it worthwhile to be the editor of this rare material, and all who have possessed these volumes endorse his judgment.

> This is a magnificent two-volume set, calculated to stir the soul and to find a place of honour and affection in every Christian who loves to read the thrilling history of the Scottish church! (SINCLAIR B. FERGUSON)

SCOTTISH PURITANS: SELECT BIOGRAPHIES
Two-Vol. Set ISBN 978-1-84871-016-0
568 & 552pp. Clothbound

For more details of all Banner publications,
including our Puritan Paperback series and
our reprints of the works of the Puritans,
please visit our website:

www.banneroftruth.co.uk

THE BANNER OF TRUTH TRUST

3 Murrayfield Road,  P O Box 621, Carlisle,
Edinburgh EH12 6EL   PA 17013,
UK   USA

www.banneroftruth.co.uk